Process Mining

Celonis Special Edition

by Steve Kaelble

for
dummies®
A Wiley Brand

Process Mining For Dummies®, Celonis Special Edition

Published by
John Wiley & Sons, Inc.
111 River St.
Hoboken, NJ 07030-5774
www.wiley.com

For general information on our other products and services, or how to create a custom *For Dummies* book for your business or organization, please contact our Business Development Department in the U.S. at 877-409-4177, contact info@dummies.biz, or visit www.wiley.com/go/custompub. For information about licensing the *For Dummies* brand for products or services, contact BrandedRights&Licenses@Wiley.com.

ISBN 978-1-119-86049-5 (pbk); ISBN 978-1-119-86050-1 (ebk);

Printed and bound by CPI Group (UK) Ltd, Croydon, CR0 4YY

Publisher's Acknowledgments

Development Editor:
Rachael Chilvers

Project Editor:
Saikarthick Kumarasamy

Acquisitions Editor: Ashley Coffey

Editorial Manager: Rev Mengle

Business Development Representative: Molly Daugherty

Project Coordinator: Melissa Cossell

Introduction

Your enterprise exists to bring to the world a specific menu of products or services. Your ability to do that successfully depends on how well you execute all of the various processes required to connect with your customers, get them to order what you're selling, create that product or service, deliver it, send out the invoice, and collect the payment. Those core processes, plus countless more. It's incredibly complicated.

What makes it even more complicated is the fact that many of these processes take place inside multiple computer applications, operated by employees in numerous departments. How can you really know whether your complicated processes are as good as they need to be? Even if you're aware of some pain in the process, how do you diagnose and treat it?

Process mining is an increasingly powerful answer to that question. As its name implies, it's all about digging for something of value — the data that can lead to the solutions you need to succeed.

It's an x-ray of your business processes that can reveal the source of process pain, whether you're aware of that pain or not. Process mining sifts through process data that can be found in all of your various transactional systems, from ERP to CRM to SCM and whatever other acronyms you want to throw its way. It provides visibility that generates insights that lead to powerful improvements in business execution.

Through process mining and its sibling task mining, your organization can gain visibility into complex processes that can otherwise be nearly impossible to see and understand. Because that view is based on data, not human observation, it's objective. It's a fact-based window into how processes are working, where and why they aren't, what's causing deviations and bottlenecks, and how that impacts your KPIs.

But that's just the beginning of a happy story. Combine the data and intelligence from process mining with actions and automations, and you can transform how your business operations are executed. This new approach to execution management can be your enterprise's ticket to a prosperous future.

About this Book

Process Mining For Dummies, Celonis Special Edition, is your introduction to this remarkable way of operating your business. Read on and you'll learn how you can use this tool for transformative process visibility and improvement. You'll learn how it works, why it matters, and how it's so much more powerful than the traditional process improvement approaches that have led up to this point.

This book spells out the steps in the process mining approach, then explores what you can do with the insights that process mining delivers. It shares how process mining discoveries can lead to greater efficiency, quality, and automation, along with lower costs.

It also spotlights how process mining plays a key role in execution management systems, through which your organization can truly transform how it operates. By ingesting real-time data, mining and analyzing for insights, planning and simulating improvements, and adopting powerful new action flows, your organization can master business execution like never before.

And fear not, this is more than just a fanciful theoretical concept. This book wraps up with tips on making it all happen right now in your organization, adopting process mining and execution management for a more successful today and tomorrow. You'll learn how to assess your company's process maturity, pick a vendor, and carefully evaluate the tools at your disposal.

Foolish Assumptions

What's your interest in process mining? In writing this book, we have made a few assumptions about you, the reader:

>> You're working for a decent-size enterprise, in any industry, and you have an interest in improving specific business processes.

>> Your role may involve process excellence, perhaps analytics, maybe IT, or you might be a line-of-business leader in an area like finance or procurement.

>> You'd appreciate some easy-to-digest insights into the magic of process mining and execution management.

Icons Used in This Book

Take a look in the margins of this book and you'll see some icons. They're there to catch your attention and let you know that something important can be found in the adjacent paragraph.

REMEMBER This book isn't terribly lengthy, but we know your time is tight. If you don't have time for every single word, at the very least don't miss the paragraphs marked with this icon.

TIP The aim here is to provide you with background, insights, and actionable advice. This icon puts the spotlight on tips you may find helpful.

TECHNICAL STUFF We've tried to sort through the technicalities to make this an easier read, but for those who like techie details, here's a paragraph for you.

WARNING What could go wrong? If we're talking about core processes (and we are), the stakes are high. This icon points out potential troubles you'll want to avoid.

Beyond the Book

Like we said, this book is full of high-level insights and intriguing concepts, but we recognize it's far from the last word on process mining. In fact, you're likely to come away from this with a thirst for additional information on the topic.

Please check the following resources for more details about process mining, execution management, and how it all can work for your enterprise.

Celonis: Ultimate Guide to Process Mining: https://www.celonis.com/ultimate-guide/

Celonis: The State of Process Excellence: https://www.celonis.com/report/state-of-process/read/

Celonis: The Process Mining Buyer's Guide: https://www.celonis.com/ebook/process-mining-buyers-guide/

Celonis: Process Mining for Procure-to-Pay: https://www.celonis.com/ebook/procure-to-pay-process/?utm_campaign=process_mining

Celonis: Process Mining for Order-to-Cash: https://www.celonis.com/ebook/process-mining-order-to-cash/?utm_campaign=process_mining

Process Excellence Network Guide: What is Process Mining?: https://www.processexcellencenetwork.com/process-mining/articles/what-is-process-mining

Gartner: Market Guide for Process Mining: https://www.celonis.com/analyst-reports/gartner-market-guide-2021/

Forrester Consulting: Trends in Process: https://www.celonis.com/analyst-reports/forrester-process-trends

Chapter **1**

Understanding Process Mining

Your business would be nowhere without employing good processes. Heck, you wouldn't even get out of the house in the morning without following processes. This chapter explains the importance of processes and the need to always improve them. It defines process and task mining. It also details why process mining is so important, and how it's a major upgrade from past process improvement approaches.

Realizing the Importance of Processes

It's so basic that it almost goes without saying: Your business wouldn't get anything done without processes. In fact, the very definition of a process is *the way something gets done*. A process is the series of steps that are taken in a particular order to achieve a specific result.

For plenty of common processes, the details don't especially matter. You expect your employees to wear shoes to work, but who cares which one they put on first? Some processes are important but uncommon, such as negotiating the lease on your office, which happens only now and then.

Other processes are both super-common and super-important. Take procurement, or purchase-to-pay. For most businesses, it happens all the time that someone needs to request a product or a service, purchase it, receive it, pay for it, and account for the whole activity from beginning to end. That is a process, with multiple steps.

For those in the sales department, there's a lead-to-order process. First your salespeople need to acquire a lead, then they must make contact, then go through a series of actions to get that potential customer to place an order.

That, in turn, triggers another process, often known as order-to-cash. What happens between the time a customer places an order and the time your business receives payment? Depending on what your business does, there may be manufacturing involved, or wholesale acquisition of a product, in either case followed by delivery and, at some point in the process, collection of payment. Instead of a physical product, you may be delivering a service. Whatever the deal, order-to-cash is what your business lives to accomplish.

If your business has a significant customer support function, you likely have processes for incident resolution. There's a way to learn from the customer that a problem exists, then a way to investigate the issue, determine a solution, and resolve the problem.

And few businesses can make any of these things happen without information technology. There are also all kinds of processes within the IT department itself, such as IT service management and application development, or even system migration, which is the process of moving the processes themselves from an old system to a new one.

All that said, for just about any desired result, there are multiple ways to make it happen. If two people set out with the same end goal in mind, it's likely that they'll follow different processes in order to get there. It isn't necessarily a matter of one process being right and the other one wrong, though there's a decent chance one is more efficient than the other, maybe faster, perhaps with less potential for error or waste along the way.

It's in the best interest of the business to standardize the most common, high-volume processes. That's how you ensure things are getting done in the best way possible, it makes it easier to determine when things are going awry, and it facilitates your ability to train new or existing employees in the best way to do their jobs.

It also just about goes without saying that there's always room for improvement. No matter how good a process is, there are ways to make it better. Processes are nearly always subject to change, either formally or on the creative whim of a problem-solver.

A BRIEF HISTORY OF PROCESSES

Processes have been around since the dawn of time, and humans have been giving serious thought to processes for more than a century and a half. One of the early big names in process thinking was an American mechanical engineer named Frederick Taylor, who pioneered a concept known as *scientific management*.

Taylor was so influential, in fact, that his theories became known as Taylorism, which reached its peak influence in the 1910s. His work was all about finding and creating the most economically efficient workflows, in particular to boost labor productivity.

Around that same time, Henry Ford was pioneering the concept of mass production in the automotive business. His first assembly line slashed the time required to build a car, which was achieved by standardizing one process after another, and lining them all up sequentially in a factory.

Car manufacturing continued to be a hotbed for process thinking in the years that followed, with more innovations happening at Toyota. The company built on the ideas of Taylor and Ford, refining new concepts of process efficiency that ultimately became known as *lean manufacturing*.

Efficiency is one key goal of process improvement. Reduction of errors and defects is another, and that's the fundamental purpose of the practice known as *Six Sigma*. This one got its start at Motorola in the 1980s, and its name comes from statistical modeling language. If you don't speak that language, just know that Six Sigma is about reducing process variability to the point that defects are really, really rare.

Your business needs to be able to figure out exactly what's happening in its processes: where things are getting stuck, and what is working best.

Improving Processes

Process thinking has evolved from an academic pursuit to a business-critical concept. And while it got its start on the factory floor (see the nearby sidebar), it now impacts businesses of all kinds. In many competitive environments, getting really good at understanding and improving processes makes all the difference between success and failure.

Think of Amazon as an example. When the company introduced same-day shipping, it set a new high bar in the world of online shopping. Amazon's mastery of the processes behind order management and delivery is its biggest differentiator.

What hasn't changed throughout all this history is the reason for formalizing processes. Repeatable processes exist to enable three key objectives:

>> Reduce the time it takes to deliver products and services to customers.

>> Reduce the cost of delivering those products and services externally and internally, while driving out waste.

>> Improve the quality of the products or services that are delivered, to be more competitive and increase customer satisfaction.

TIP

The other thing that hasn't changed is the importance of continually improving these processes. Here are some of the fundamental ways of changing processes to make them better:

>> **Standardizing:** Making the process as repeatable as possible, and ensuring that the process as-is matches the process as-designed.

>> **Streamlining:** Removing redundant or unnecessary activities from the process.

>> **Optimizing:** Reengineering the process to produce more value, such as improving quality or reducing costs.

>> **Automating:** Removing aspects of the process that require human efforts.

Defining Process Mining

Process improvement of the kind described in the preceding section is a true art. Depending on the process you're studying, it can be quite an involved endeavor to examine, document, and map out the various steps, then pinpoint and eliminate pain points. The good news is, the whole process of process improvement is, in and of itself, always continuing to improve.

REMEMBER

The intriguing improvement that this book is about is known as *process mining*. It's helpful to think about it like an x-ray of your business processes; an exceptional way to understand core processes, locate the inefficiencies, and take steps to remove gaps.

What makes process mining possible is the fact that so many of our most prevalent business processes are conducted by way of information systems. In the general sense, mining involves seeking and extracting something of value, such as diamonds from a diamond mine. Process mining extracts valuable knowledge from the event logs that information systems produce.

Within your time-stamped event logs, you'll find a goldmine of detail about every step and every deviation in the process. For example, the process of dealing with a purchase order will include events such as when the purchase order (PO) was created, when it was approved, fulfilled, and dispatched.

What's valuable about the information in those event logs is the ability to piece them together and visualize business processes as they run. Just as important, as mentioned above, there's often more than one way to get something done, and the event logs reveal all of the variations in those processes.

Let's stop to think for a minute about how monumental those process variations can be. Consider the accounts payable process as an example. One study found that the cost per invoice averaged

$17.42, but the best-in-class performer could achieve the same result for just $6.84 per invoice. If you could get an x-ray of your process and figure out how to reduce that cost for the hundreds or thousands of invoices your company processes every year, you could save a small fortune.

Run the same kind of exercise in accounts receivable. Would it surprise you to learn that one study found an average metric of 29.9 days delinquent? What if an x-ray of your AR process identified the key ways your process varies from the best-in-class that averages just eight days? When it comes to collecting your bills, time certainly is money.

Now, you could certainly go about making these kinds of improvements through some of the older approaches to process improvement, but process mining is most definitely an upgrade. Here are some of the benefits:

>> **It's objective:** Process mining offers fact-based insights that come from actual data. You can audit and analyze that data to improve your existing processes.

>> **It's faster and more accurate:** Process mining replaces process mapping, which is much more manual, more tedious, and more subjective. It's a whole lot speedier and cheaper, and its objectivity increases its accuracy.

>> **It avoids the rip-and-replace:** Process mining works with your existing systems. Think of it as a "layer" above your IT infrastructure.

To really understand how it works, it's instructive to ponder the basic concept of what a process is. As mentioned in passing toward the beginning of this chapter, a process is a series of actions or steps running from a starting point to a recognized finish. These steps can be repeated, and they can be improved upon in the hopes of getting from start to finish in the most efficient and consistent way possible.

When these steps take place in a transactional system, they leave a digital footprint in the form of event log data. Process mining extracts that data and uses it to create a living picture of what processes actually look like in practice.

It's important to realize that what a process actually looks like may or may not match the way that process was originally defined. Processes tend to change over time, and no matter how well-planned they once were, they can easily go astray. And as time goes on, deviations in the path can become the rule, not the exception.

TIP

Beyond that, there are also changes forced by evolving customer expectations, new product lines, changes in geographic markets, and all kinds of other factors that can impact how well an existing process works. The ability to efficiently update and fix processes depends on getting full, real-time visibility into how the processes are working.

Employing Task Mining

By now you may be thinking, process mining certainly sounds great — but what about those processes or steps that happen outside of transactional systems? In such cases, there are no event logs to mine. Are you out of luck?

Nope. That's where a related endeavor known as *task mining* comes into play. Task mining employs technology to collect user desktop data. Together with process mining, it helps your organization gain the fullest possible view into how processes run.

As mentioned in the previous section, your event logs tell you when a purchase order was created and approved; when it was fulfilled and dispatched. But it doesn't include some of the details that happened on the computer desktop where that work took place.

Someone filled in the PO, checked the amounts to be sure they were accurate, and matched receipts with invoices. That activity happened outside of the system that actually handles the POs, but it's highly important for understanding the PO process. Task mining puts those insights into the mix (and can add in some ancillary insights such as the fact that the worker had to spend a lot of time digging through emails to find all the information needed to complete the PO task).

It takes some nifty tricks and technologies to collect this task mining information. Task mining leverages optical character recognition technology, or OCR. It employs natural language processing, or NLP. And it's aided by machine-learning algorithms to help it really understand the actions people are taking on their desktops and find the patterns that are impacting business outcomes.

REMEMBER

Here are the basics of how it works. Task mining:

>> **Captures desktop data:** We're talking clicks and scrolls and other actions, screenshots, and time stamps.

>> **Adds in the business context:** This is where OCR comes in, collecting all the text and numbers on the screen to put what's happening into context.

>> **Clusters activities:** NLP and artificial intelligence technologies gain an understanding of each action and cluster actions into overarching activities that they're a part of.

>> **Matches business data:** Identifying information allows the task mining software to correlate what the user is doing with specific business data in operational systems, which is how you really figure out how actions are impacting business outcomes.

>> **Optimizes the process:** All of these insights can then be harnessed to optimize processes and boost business performance through the use of an execution management system.

REMEMBER

The technologies are safe and secure. And they include advanced privacy features to ensure that sensitive data remains hidden, only relevant user interaction data is captured, and only approved people can see the user interaction data.

Understanding Why Process Mining Matters

Was life simpler in the old days? Was it better? It's an age-old argument between generations that may never be resolved. As for core business processes, it's safe to say that they were simpler back in the day. They're arguably better today, but the more digitized they've become, the more complex.

Indeed, business evolution has really made the process environment increasingly challenging to get a handle on. Process mapping has provided lots of benefit through the years, but it's more vital than ever to have a really holistic understanding of the process landscape.

Here's why process mining is so consequential:

>> **You get complete visibility into processes:** It offers a 100% objective, real-time look that's based on IT data.

>> **You can quantify the impact:** With a better understanding of process gaps, you can demonstrate value before and after you put a fix in place.

>> **You can get stakeholders onboard:** With data-driven solution suggestions that even have return-on-investment (ROI) attached, it's much easier to get buy-in and alignment.

>> **You can set priorities:** Understanding the impact that specific process gaps have on business outcomes helps you prioritize your energy and resources. Don't just pick the low-hanging fruit — go for the tastiest!

>> **You can quickly achieve value:** Compared with previous incarnations of process improvement, process mining is easy and fast to implement, which means you'll demonstrate the value much more quickly.

That's the lowdown on the value process mining brings. Task mining matters for a number of additional reasons that make it beneficial to just about any enterprise:

>> You uncover inefficiencies in work patterns outside of transactional systems.

>> You become better able to measure and optimize workforce productivity.

>> You can link manual processes with your enterprise business processes, driving next-best-actions across the desktop.

Ultimately, both process mining and task mining have a lot to offer, and the combination is especially powerful. You can apply both concepts to all kinds of processes, from procurement to payables, and from managing orders to handling receivables.

Upgrading from Older Approaches

Thinking back to the challenge of making processes as good as they can be, remember that today's processes in the real world often don't match the way they were envisioned to be. There can be huge differences between what you can view as the *assumed process* — which is the way the process was conceived (and the way a lot of process owners and managers think it still is) — and the *as-is process*, which is the way the process really plays out.

These gaps aren't necessarily anyone's fault. They're simply the product of the evolution and advances in how business operates. For decades now, companies have been building processes and running operations inside of rigid, fragmented transactional systems.

Accounts payable may, for example, run through multiple IT systems operated by a variety of users in different departments. How can anyone really gain visibility into a situation like this? Older process improvement approaches, as valuable as they've been through the years, really can't get a handle on this challenge.

Consider the traditional process mapping exercise. Interviews with process owners and managers aim to paint a picture of what's going on in the process. There may be whiteboards involved, and countless sticky notes. A lot of people have a hand in the exercise.

WARNING

To be sure, it's possible to gain some value from this kind of endeavor. But you're relying on a lot of people's opinions that may be subjective and partial. And the effort is so long and involved that by the time it's finished and the results analyzed, the process may have changed already. It's a one-time understanding of the process, and it'll be stale before you know it.

Process mining, on the other hand, relies on data for an objective and complete view. Observations are immediate and self-service, so corrective actions can be made quickly. And it's ongoing, continually enhancing your understanding of processes and how they can be better.

Chapter **2**

Exploring How Process Mining Works

rocess mining gives you an amazing ability to look under the hood of your company's business processes and really see how they work. How? This chapter gives more detail on the steps involved, from ingesting the data, to illustrating and analyzing the processes, to comparing your metrics with others, to seeing if your processes are working the way you intended.

Ingesting the Data

As Chapter 1 explained, business processes these days are quite complex. They are highly digitized, taking place inside a wide range of information systems. If your organization is like many, your processes may operate across different systems crunching different kinds of data, run by a big roster of people who are working across multiple departments.

But take a step back and consider an individual business object, or case, working its way through one of those complicated processes. It's moving through these information systems and leaving behind digital clues. These clues are records of each brief stop along the path of this business process, whether it's an invoice on the way from creation to payment, or a customer service ticket being submitted and eventually resolved.

You might think of these clues as being like the proverbial breadcrumbs left along the path in the Brothers Grimm's "Hansel and Gretel." The difference is, these breadcrumbs don't get eaten by birds, but instead serve a very useful purpose. Come to think of it, that's a rather gruesome fairytale — perhaps it's more pleasant to imagine these clues as digital footprints in the sand.

REMEMBER

Better yet, just think of them as events in the process. The digital records of these events are known as *event logs*, and they're exceptionally valuable collections of data.

TECHNICAL STUFF

Getting a detailed look at your process through process mining means your tools need to get at that event data, and there are a number of ways that can happen. One way is to export an event log from the system, giving you a comma-separated values file that the process mining tool can import. That's certainly fine, but the most advanced process mining efforts use real-time data ingestion, which is constantly syncing the latest process data.

What kinds of information is contained in these event logs? At the very least, three important pieces of process data for each individual event are in the log:

>> **Case ID:** This is a unique reference identifying each business object.

>> **Activity:** This describes the stage of the process that the case has just gone through.

>> **Timestamp:** This records the precise time the case went through that stage in the process.

Take a look at Figure 2-1 to see what this can look like.

Many event logs have more details than just these three key tidbits of information. Perhaps there are details about the vendor involved, or if it's a service ticket, it might include a priority level.

Process information is stored in **event logs**

CASE ID	ACTIVITY	TIMESTAMP
101	Create Order	04-29-2020 09:34:55
101	Approve Credit	04-29-2020 10:54:33
101	Create Delivery	04-30-2020 12:34:19
101	Ship Order	04-30-2020 18:54:38
201	Create Order	04-29-2020 09:34:55
202	Change Price	04-29-2020 09:34:55
203	Create Delivery	04-29-2020 09:34:55
204	Ship Order	04-29-2020 09:34:55
N01	Create Order	03-15-2020 11:34:55
N02	Create Delivery	03-15-2020 12:22:57
N03	Change Quantity	03-15-2020 16:34:17
N04	Create Delivery	03-16-2020 02:15:09

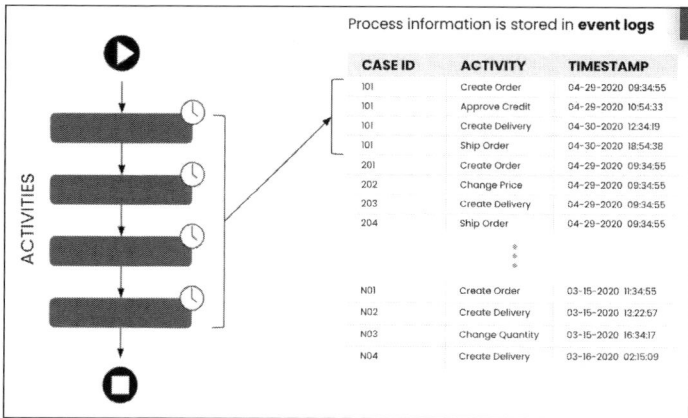

FIGURE 2-1: Key process data in the event log.

Making Process Discovery Happen

The process mining tool has now gathered together a bunch of event log data. Now is when the real action begins, as the tool begins to sift through the data to see what riches can be mined.

REMEMBER

The stage known as *process discovery* involves using the event logs to create an end-to-end visualization of the process. It follows every step that every case took as it moved through the cycle, from beginning to end. It superimposes all of those journeys into one visualization, a chronological sequence of events from the start to the finish. Some people refer to this as a *digital twin*.

Remember that there are different ways to get from here to there, variations in the path that a process might follow. Maybe most of those footprints in the sand are pretty much in the same place for each case, but now and then a path takes a step to the left or right.

In process mining, those slightly different paths from beginning to end are known as *variants*. There may be hundreds or thousands of different variants that show up on the process map that the mining tool creates.

REMEMBER

It's a fact of life that variants happen — it's not unexpected, and it isn't in and of itself a problem. Take a look at Figure 2-2 for a very simple glimpse into how two different variants can combine into one superimposed process map. There's a price change in the second variant, and it shows up as a potential side path on the combined map.

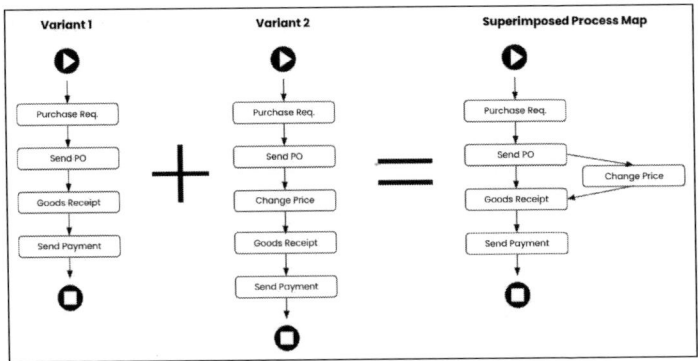

FIGURE 2-2: A simple superimposed process map.

It's also true that some variants, well, vary more than others. Those that don't seem to follow the standard or accepted path are known as *deviations*.

Now, for a more real-world look at what process discovery can look like, check out Figure 2-3. This is an image generated by Celonis process mining technology, zoomed out to show all of the many variants. Illustrate enough variants and deviations and it starts to look like a plate of spaghetti.

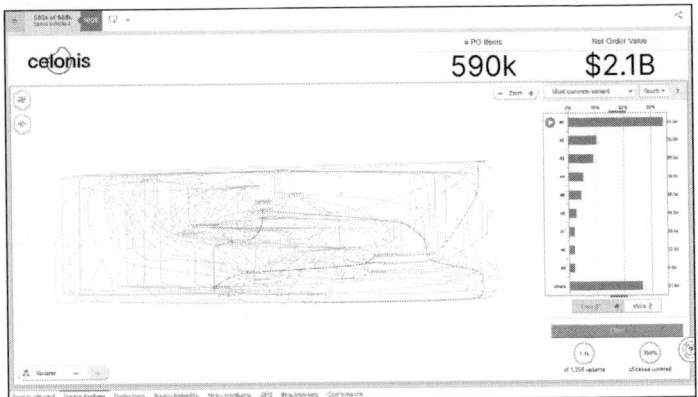

FIGURE 2-3: The "spaghetti diagram" process map.

And now one more picture. Figure 2-4 shows the Celonis process visualization zoomed in to show what's known as the *happy path*. This is the most efficient-looking of the various possibilities, a straight line that's the way one would imagine a good process ought to look like — and one would hope this is the most common variant.

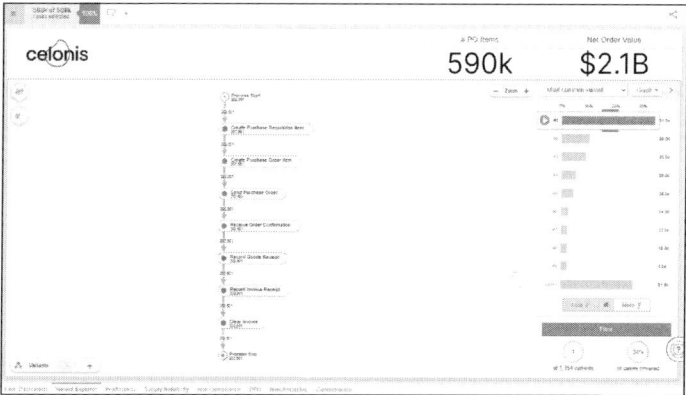

FIGURE 2-4: The happy path process map.

Analyzing Processes

Of course, if every process invariably followed an efficient, straight-line happy path, there wouldn't be much point in process mining. But in the real world, problems and inefficiencies are commonplace, and there's always room to improve. The *process analytics* step of process mining is where you start to dig into the root causes of process inefficiencies and quantify how they're impacting your key performance indicators.

As the analysis digs into the causes of process inefficiencies, here are some of the questions that you're asking:

>> Where are the bottlenecks in the process?

>> What is causing some cases to run late?

>> Which resources are overloaded?

>> Which activities are skipped most often?

>> Which resources create deviations?

As for quantifying the impact of variants and inefficiencies, you might be asking these kinds of questions:

>> How does this particular variant impact a certain process KPI, such as operational cost?

>> How does automation shorten the process cycle time?

>> What percentage of steps in the process are automated?

>> What percentage of cases are following the established process, and what's the percentage that don't conform?

TIP   A helpful tool enables you to really filter and drill down into the data to test any assumptions you have about inefficiencies. But it also can explore the process as it is and find inefficiencies on its own through the power of AI and machine learning.

Benchmarking Processes

As you build up your wealth of process information through process mining, you can start to compare process performance across different dimensions. That can help you pinpoint stellar performers or identify problem points, and ultimately apply lessons and best practices from one place to another — across teams, business units, or geographies, for example.

You could check your processes in different countries, perhaps comparing the time it takes to process an invoice in one place versus the other. You could also check the throughput time of a purchase order from one supplier, compared with another. Figure 2-5 shows a Celonis dashboard comparing process performance between two countries.

FIGURE 2-5: Process benchmarking.

Checking Conformance

Conformance checking is the part of process mining where you can really start to see the difference between the way you think your process ought to be and the way it really is in practice. You gain the ability to define the preferred path, then see how processes are deviating from the path.

Earlier we referred to the assumed process versus the as-is process. Conformance checking gauges where your as-is truly is, and what percentage of your cases really do conform to the desired process. That helps you determine when steps are being executed in the wrong order, or perhaps skipped entirely. And you can see exactly when things are taking longer than expected at certain stages of the process.

REMEMBER

Not to be too much of a downer, there's a glass-half-full way of looking at conformance checking. You are, after all, trying to make improvements in the process. As you do so, your conformance checking will show you the progress you're making, giving you proof that more cases are running through the process in the most optimal manner.

Figure 2-6 gets this point across. It's an example of conformance checking, and the way you want to see the curve moving.

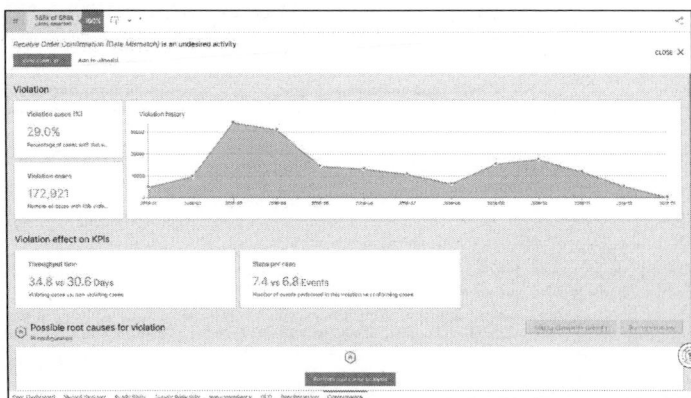

FIGURE 2-6: Conformance checking.

Chapter **3**

Making the Most of Process Mining

As powerful as process mining's insights can be, they're only truly valuable if they inform the way your business operates. This chapter describes how process mining fits into a bigger picture of business execution. It shows how insights can lead to real improvements in business performance, and how artificial intelligence and machine learning can help keep the transformation rolling. And it outlines how an execution management system can bring all of these powers together for the greatest impact.

Turning Insights into Automation

Automation certainly seems like a Holy Grail of process improvement and enterprise productivity. Given that human capital is among your enterprise's biggest expenses, any way you can reduce human effort within a process workflow is going to be an exciting opportunity.

Some might think this is a way to reduce your staffing level, but that's not necessarily the point. When it comes to automation, the first priority for most companies is to augment their employees' work so they can be more productive. Indeed, research conducted by Celonis found that respondents' top goal for process improvement is "increase productivity," not "reduce costs."

One way automation helps employees get more done is by reducing the time it takes to complete a process. As for other key measures such as reducing waste, improving quality, and cutting costs, when done well, automation can boost those important metrics, too.

REMEMBER

All that sounds great, but the reality is, most enterprises are barely scratching the surface when it comes to automating processes. One McKinsey survey found that two-thirds of respondents were giving it a shot, but of those, only about a sixth had really succeeded in fully automating a process. About the same share had gone all-in on an automation program that could scale automation technologies across multiple parts of the business.

One of the big reasons this evolution has been so slow is that enterprise systems are so complex and fragmented, and there's not much visibility into how things really work. That makes it incredibly challenging to identify which areas of a process are the best candidates for automation.

WARNING

Just as important, those dynamics make it hard to know the best way to automate the process. Automation can reduce waste and increase efficiency, but that's not a given. If you take a process that's broken or inefficient and automate it, all you've found is a way to do something badly, but do it faster. And if you hard-code automations into your systems, you might end up having to re-code them every time the process changes.

This is a common pitfall when it comes to certain types of automation, such as *robotic process automation*. RPA bots are great at automating simple data-entry tasks, but they're not highly intelligent or flexible, so when other circumstances in the process change, RPA automations don't always change with it. That causes things to break.

That's where process mining comes into the picture. When undertaken in advance of automation, process mining can add value in multiple ways. It helps find the right solution for fixing process issues, which isn't always automation. It also sheds light on which parts of a process are exceptional candidates for automation.

In short, process mining and automation go together like peanut butter and jelly, or strawberries and chocolate. The sum of the parts really is a lot better than either component on its own. Automation for automation's sake isn't worth much, but process mining insights also aren't worth much if you don't fully act on them.

As those annoying TV commercials proclaim, "but wait, there's more!" Process mining can add in not just the all-important insights, but also incredibly valuable oversight. You're best off when process mining not only informs the creation of your automation, but also monitors its implementation in order to continually improve it. That's where automation based on artificial intelligence and machine learning can really change this game. It yields a system flexible enough to adapt and learn over time.

The ultimate point here is, making the most of process mining means using its insights to their maximum potential. It's great on its own, but truly transformative when part of a platform that powers all facets of business execution. It's not just a now-and-then tool for process improvement, but an ongoing part of the most effective daily business operations.

Adopting Execution Management

That idea, as described in the previous paragraph, isn't simply a science-fiction dream, but a present-day reality known as *execution management*. More and more successful businesses are tapping into this kind of transformative platform that brings all of these capabilities to bear.

Early in this book, we described process mining as sort of an x-ray of your business processes. That's a reasonable description, but when you think about it, in the world of medicine, an x-ray is only one step in the process of getting better. The x-ray image helps you learn what's wrong and where — but then you must take other steps to heal, whether it's setting a broken bone or surgically removing a tumor.

Similarly, the data you gather through process mining isn't just for looking at and admiring. You need that data to move your business forward, inform decisions, drive actions, improve performance, and power day-to-day execution. An execution management system (EMS) adds a brain to your operational landscape, helping you decide which remedies can heal your operational challenges.

REMEMBER

Process mining is the gateway to execution management. An execution management system, such as that created by Celonis, transforms how companies run day-to-day operations, serve customers, run financial processes, operate the supply chain, and much more. Here are the five core capabilities you should expect from a powerful EMS:

>> **Real-time data ingestion:** The EMS must connect in real time to all process data, from all varieties of sources and applications.

>> **Process and task mining:** Through this step, the EMS creates the treasure map that pinpoints where your enterprise can achieve value through transformed processes. The best technology can mine across multiple processes to combine even more powerful insights.

>> **Planning and simulation:** The EMS must be able to look ahead with process modeling capabilities, simulating how changes in business practices will impact outcomes, and help you chart a course from your current as-is process to your desired to-be process.

>> **Visual and daily management:** The EMS should provide tools for building easy, customizable interfaces that bring insights and observations to players all across the enterprise, allowing them to monitor process KPIs and take action instantly.

>> **Action flows:** Execution is all about actions, so the EMS should provide action flows to execute and automate across all underlying systems. And it should be able to do so in a way that's low-code and easy to use.

TIP

While you want to make sure your EMS checks all of these boxes from a technical perspective, also be sure it can fit these capabilities into your business function's specific needs. The right EMS provider has apps or packages that are pre-configured for the processes you want to use it with, whether that's selling, shipping, collecting, buying, or paying. An EMS uses powerful, ongoing insights to keep your execution actions fresh.

Chapter **4**

Seeing Process Mining in Action

P rocess mining certainly sounds like a fantastic concept. But in real-life terms, how can it help your organization truly get better at everything you set out to do? This chapter explores a variety of use cases to see what you can achieve through process mining, intelligent analysis, and the kinds of operational enhancements that come from the implementation of a great execution management system.

Improving Core Functions

Your organization buys stuff. You have to pay for that stuff. You sell products or services. That may involve shipping something out. And you need to collect payments from your customers. All pretty basic, really, but each of these functions relies on super-critical processes.

If you're like a lot of people, you've gotten pretty good at managing processes with the tools at hand, as well as working to improve. In some cases, that means mapping and capturing processes with spreadsheet software, maybe a presentation app or a diagramming tool.

WARNING

That older approach to process improvement, though, is quite time consuming and labor intensive. Just capturing the information to map involves a lot of people, gathered in meetings or work sessions or interviews. They scratch their heads and remember details about how things work, they interject their opinions and theories, you map, and then you try to figure out the lessons and solutions.

REMEMBER

Process mining is a real game-changer. It takes over much of that hands-on work, removes the subjectivity, and gets incredibly insightful information straight from your transactional systems. And then the execution management system of which it is a part offers keen insights and AI-informed solutions, helping you make smart decisions and take the best actions.

Order-to-Cash Use Cases

Getting the order-to-cash process right is absolutely vital to the success of your organization. As with so many pieces of the operational puzzle, this process touches lots of other pieces. Order-to-cash has everything to do with order management and accounts receivable, but is also deeply integrated with sales, finance, and supply chain operations.

Crucially, these are areas where many businesses stumble. Consider order management, for example. On-time delivery rate is a big key performance indicator (KPI) in this area, and while top performers get the job done 90% of the time or more, the State of Business Execution Benchmarks Report finds that the average company is on-time just under 43% of the time. In the all-important arena of customer satisfaction, the average company measures 69%, while top performers often are greater than 90%.

Also consider accounts receivable. On KPIs for days sales outstanding, top performers hit about 24 days, while the average company is at 53. The best companies are at about 8 when it comes to average days delinquent, while a typical company is almost 30 days.

Improving order management

Let's take a look at how process mining can help out with order management. Here are some KPI areas where problems are common, with some thoughts about why they happen and how process mining and execution management solve the problem.

Inventory management

Your aim is to keep stock as low as possible, but be there faithfully for everything that production and fulfillment requires, while avoiding supply chain pitfalls. Execution management can help identify patterns related to late supply deliveries, and automatically tweak lead times.

Your system can also update reorder points based on changes in demand. And it can fix problems with inaccurate equipment tracking.

On-time delivery

Your process mining effort may identify a process gap in the area of credit checks, which are often taking too long and slowing down order processing. You discover that even your regular customers who have a great history of paying on-time are having their orders held up for credit approval.

TIP

Machine learning, of the kind available from the Celonis solution, can predict which customers are most likely to pay on time. For those good customers, you can safely skip the credit check and speed up their orders by days.

Cost per order

Process mining may find a bunch of manual rework caused by incorrect price information. That rework raises the cost per order. A deeper dive into the findings reveals that some of the master data is out-of-date.

There's a solution for that, too. Your execution management system should be able to spot those inconsistencies in contract pricing, and automatically fix the pricing according to the correct contract.

Net promoter score

This metric is wildly important, because it's about getting positive word-of-mouth from your customers. They're not so positive if they get an order confirmation with a delivery date, and then the delivery date gets changed.

If your process mining expedition identifies that problem, your execution management system should provide a solution. Typically, delivery dates are based on standard lead times, but supply chain issues can mess up the ability to meet those standards. An intelligent execution management system can spot areas likely to be affected by supply chain issues, and either automatically provide a more realistic delivery date, or escalate the order to a manager who can find a way to expedite it.

Fixing accounts receivable

Now let's take a look at similar issues in the world of accounts receivable. Here are some typical KPIs where things can go awry, be examined through process mining, and fixed through solutions from an execution management system.

Days sales outstanding

The process gap seems pretty straightforward: Customers are paying late. But why? Process mining identifies a failure to identify at-risk payments before they get out of hand.

The solution from execution management is to automatically identify high-risk customers based on their likelihood to pay. The potentially troublesome ones are escalated to the support team, and that escalation is flagged in the CRM.

Time to invoice

You can't get paid if you don't first send out the bill. The identified process gap here is that invoices are taking too long to create and send.

This is a job for automation by way of the execution management system. The process mining analysis finds that invoices are not being created as soon as possible after delivery. The solution is to automatically trigger invoice creation within 24 hours of goods delivery.

Perfect invoice rate

You also may not be paid if your invoice has errors, such as the wrong billing address or customer identification. Your process mining finds that invoices are sometimes using incorrect master data.

The execution management system steps in to save the day. It automatically reviews contracts and historical data to recommend appropriate updates to master data. It can either notify the master data team, or automatically modify the invoice if the confidence level is deemed high enough.

Purchase-to-Pay Use Cases

You can't sell stuff (or provide services) if you don't first acquire stuff, so it's well worth ensuring that your purchase-to-pay processes are up to speed, too.

TIP

There are two primary parts to this puzzle — procurement and accounts payable. Your improvement efforts need to look at the whole journey.

REMEMBER

No surprise that there's plenty of room for improvement here, too. Consider some of the top KPIs linked to procurement. One is spend under management. Top performers influence a full 75% of their total spend, according to the State of Business Execution Benchmarks Report. The average company, though, influences just 47%. Getting supplier deliveries on-time is vital, too. Successful companies have an 83% supplier delivery reliability metric, but the average is just 54%.

Taking a look at the other half, accounts payable, the paid-on-time rate is important if you want to maintain good relations with your most important suppliers. It's 77% for top performers, but just 50% on average. That said, companies want to keep suppliers happy while achieving a high days payable outstanding, because it means they're able to maximize working capital and make short-term investments. A good benchmark is 74.5 days, but the average is 48.4.

Improving procurement

Here's a look at how you can focus on some of the most important procurement KPIs through the sleuthing power of process mining and the solution wizardry of execution management.

Processing time of purchase requisitions

Your teams can ask for something, but the procurement process can get held up right at the starting gate. One process gap that process mining might pinpoint is a high volume of free-text requisitions. This happens when requisitioners manually create a request rather than picking a standard vendor with pre-negotiated contract terms.

The execution management solution that emerges from this process mining exercise is a machine learning model that can automatically convert a free-text purchase requisition to a PO. Or, it might recommend that the requisitioner select an item from an existing catalog rather than straying from the standard.

Inbound on-time delivery rate

Once the order has been processed, now you're at the mercy of the supplier to make the delivery on-time. In the meantime, you make plans for when the item will arrive. Process mining finds that, all too often, supplier deliveries are later than you expected. But why, and what can be done?

Analysis may show that the master data related to your internal planning parameters is not correct, causing you to make assumptions that are just not realistic. The execution management system can fix those faulty parameters to reflect reality. Or, the system might notify the planning team that there may be a systemic issue of which they're not yet aware. Either way, you're caught off-guard a lot less often.

Spend under management

The opposite of spend under management is maverick spending. Too many people are out shopping without someone looking over their shoulder to be sure they're shopping wisely. Your KPI may indicate this is a problem, but it takes some good process mining to figure out why it's happening.

Perhaps what's happening is that requisitioners are trying to speed up a purchase, or maybe buy from a preferred vendor, so they're trying to get around the established internal processes. This unmanaged spending can be costly. Execution management can notify category managers of repeat offenders, reject maverick purchases, block system access, and even contact those vendors that are repeatedly fulfilling maverick purchases.

Getting a better handle on accounts payable

This is a super-important function. As outlined earlier, the accounts payable (AP) department needs to be the master of potentially competing interests. On one hand, it needs to maintain positive supplier relationships by paying in a timely manner. But not so timely as to unnecessarily eat up working capital. Here are some prominent KPIs with thoughts on how process mining and execution management can help.

Days payable outstanding

The process gap here is payments going out earlier than necessary. Process mining may reveal that it's happening because invoices are being posted before the due date, and payment runs are moving forward with these too-early invoices included.

The execution management system resolves these issues by automatically checking and applying contracted payment terms, so that invoices don't post before they need to. It can also notify the supplier of the discrepancy, to keep relations smooth.

Paid-on-time rate

In this case, your KPI is showing too many invoices being paid late — the question is why? Process mining discovers that price changes are slowing things down. Suppliers may be using outdated prices when invoicing, and when they do, it takes extra processing time to resolve the matter.

The solution from execution management is to automatically check and apply contracted pricing. And if the suppliers have invoiced incorrectly, the system can automatically notify them, to prevent future problems and keep them in the loop.

Touchless invoice rate

You want as many invoices as possible to sail through without human intervention, but your KPI reveals a lot are not. Process mining shows there are often incorrect or missing fields, perhaps because of master data issues, or maybe errors on the part of the vendor.

Your execution management system steps in to identify discrepancies in invoice fields, comparing the PO, the invoice, and historical data. It can automatically update erroneous fields based on the PO and historical data, without bothering your humans.

Back Office and IT Use Cases

As noted earlier, process mining and execution management are made possible by the fact that your key processes take place within various applications that generate data. This activity lives in the world of IT, and it so happens that your IT teams have their own useful use cases for process mining.

System migration

IT wants to be on-time and on-budget in system migration, but that's challenging when process mapping is manual, fit-gap analysis is subjective, and user adoption is subpar. Process mining can automatically create an objective process map, visualizing every variant of every process as it actually happens in the IT systems.

With the data, the EMS can compare the as-is with the to-be, spotlight the deltas and figure out why they're happening. It can generate a ranked list of fit-gap deltas to assess. Execution management can also spot feature underutilization, so that actions can be taken to improve adoption.

IT service management

The IT team spends a lot of time fielding service tickets, and the clients it services want to get those tickets handled as quickly as possible. Process mining can help uncover inefficiencies within IT service management and figure out what to do about them.

Process mining technology can, for example, identify areas that would benefit from a *shift left* that allows solutions to happen earlier in the resolution process. It can cut down on multi-hops and find ways to resolve tickets on the first touch. It can help IT service management meet SLA requirements by opening up faster process paths. It can even spot places where a simple refund would cost less than a resolution, which saves money and reduces the backlog of service tickets.

Front Office Use Cases

Your interactions with customers are vital to your success — both during the sales process and the need for customer service. Execution management informed by process mining can make a big difference.

Sales opportunity management

Closing the deal is what your salespeople are aiming to do every day, but they may not be performing at full potential. Process mining can help boost execution capacity in a number of ways.

TIP

Machine learning, for example, can allow execution management to point sales reps in the right direction, toward opportunities that are most likely to close. The right solution can spotlight actions that close pipeline gaps and accelerate pipeline progression.

The system can also reduce the sales cycle time by removing manual steps from the quote process. And it can leverage better data for greater forecast accuracy.

Customer service

The better your customer service, the more likely it is that your customer will come back for more, as well as recommend that others patronize your business. Process mining and execution management check into your transactional systems to find out where resolution times are slowing down needlessly.

TIP

You can find out which service case attributes are linked to the greatest delays, where incidents may be handled by multiple agents, and where self-service solutions are breaking down. Improving self-service saves time for your agents and makes customers happier, and happier customers mean higher net promoter scores.

Improving Strategic Initiatives

Beyond the specific cases outlined earlier, many organizations see the value of process mining as a strategic tool to support wider-ranging initiatives. Many companies have set out enterprise-wide initiatives such as digital transformation and sustainability, and you might be surprised to learn how process mining can contribute to these efforts.

Digital transformation

Few businesses these days can ignore the critical need for digital transformation. It's a competitive world, and having the best product on the market is only part of the story. If it's easier to do business with your competitors, or faster, you may be sunk.

This is a strategic initiative for which process mining can be absolutely essential. Because digital transformation is about improving your processes, you'll never get there without first understanding your processes. You need visibility into where you are today, and process mining provides that visibility.

That current-state understanding, in fact, is what helps you build the business case for digital transformation in the first place. It becomes the benchmark on which the success of your transformation can be assessed. And it provides the roadmap for transformation in the most efficient, effective way.

Pursuing sustainability

Many organizations have placed a high priority on sustainability, and as it happens, a great place to start is within existing processes. Procurement is a big one — you need sustainable practices that cascade through the supply chain.

You'll never get there without closely following data. As noted elsewhere, process mining can play a vital role in procurement, including ensuring that your spending is targeted toward the right suppliers that you've identified in your sustainability program. In this aspect, execution management isn't just about controlling costs — it can actually ensure that you're staying on track in this important strategic aim.

Chapter **5**

Getting Started With Process Mining

I f your organization isn't yet benefiting from process mining, there's no time like the present to get started! The sooner you tap into this powerful technology, the sooner you can move your processes further toward their full potential.

This chapter outlines your game plan for going down this path. You have options to consider regarding your overall approach, and you'll benefit from some self-examination of your organization's process maturity. The good news is, you don't have to set forth on this journey alone — this chapter gives advice on assistance you can seek as you choose vendors.

Exploring Your Options

REMEMBER

The first thing to ponder is the nature of your process mining project. There are three basic options for adopting process mining, and the key to your success will be choosing the most applicable deployment approach:

>> **Standalone process mining project:** This is essentially a discovery-only approach. Your process mining expedition

collects the data and generates insights, and then your organization works to figure out what to do with those insights.

>> **Process mining enhancement approach:** In this concept, your process mining initiative is loosely connected with other initiatives. Automation, for example, can turn some of your insights into actions.

>> **Execution management system approach:** This is the most all-in concept. Process mining is embedded into a wider execution platform to help you maximize business performance on a broad scale.

According to Gartner, just under half of the process mining implementations in 2018 followed the first approach of a standalone project, but by 2020 it was down to more like a third, as more companies explored the more involved options. About two-thirds of organizations that adopted process mining in 2020 followed either the enhancement or execution management approach. It's also possible to take it a step at a time — you can start small with a single process, then expand the effort to other processes and systems.

The question is, which approach best suits your organization's needs? Keep on reading for additional insights.

Assessing Process Maturity

One key consideration as you plan your deployment is an honest assessment of where your organization is when it comes to process maturity. The further along you are in the stages outlined below, the readier you are for the full execution management approach.

REMEMBER Don't fret about where your business lands in this assessment, though. No judgment is intended, and the most important point is, your enterprise will benefit tremendously from process mining, no matter where you're starting off.

Following are some detailed thoughts about the four stages of process maturity. Your aim is to figure out which stage sounds the most like where your enterprise is at right now, then select a deployment that really fits with your level of organizational, process, and technology maturity.

Stage 1: Developing process understanding

About 65% of companies are at this point, according to the American Productivity & Quality Center. In this stage, your organization has process knowledge that's largely dispersed, and largely opinion-based.

At this point, you may be conducting whiteboarding sessions to better understand your processes. You may be manually mapping processes, which is a great start, but you're probably finding it rather slow and tedious — so much so that by the time you get a process fully examined, it has already evolved into something else. As for key performance indicators (KPIs), you have them, but they tend to be siloed across fragmented systems.

TIP Where does process mining fit in for enterprises at this level of process maturity? It's a fantastic way to develop a greater understanding of processes, and it's a whole lot faster and easier.

Stage 2: Standardizing processes

About 20% of companies have gained some decent process understanding and are now working on boosting their process standardization. Established process owners are in place, as well as targets that these owners are working toward. In fact, KPIs have been consolidated into end-to-end metrics, with more integrated reporting.

TIP By this stage, your standardization is benefiting from a more objective view into process gaps. Implement process mining here and you'll be well on the way to even greater standardization.

Stage 3: Optimizing processes

About 10% of companies have hit this next level of process maturity, where outcomes are really starting to show the benefit. Process champions have emerged, with an aim of truly impacting and improving outcomes.

REMEMBER In Stage 3, your organization is implementing process-specific optimizations. From a technology perspective, you have deployed and integrated digital point solutions. You'll really benefit from process mining here, too, as it will continue to drive even greater optimization.

Stage 4: Innovating process execution

There's strong integration between insights and innovative actions by the time you hit this highest level of maturity (but only about 5% of companies are here now, according to APQC). By this point, your organization has implemented a full center of excellence approach to driving execution capacity.

REMEMBER You're benefiting from intelligent actions and automations across processes. Your organization has added more and more enterprise systems, but your technology now includes an intelligent layer on top of them, connecting systems and solutions. By this stage, process mining is an integral part of your daily business operations.

Seeking Assistance

Process mining is among the fastest-growing categories of enterprise software. More than half of the Fortune 500 is already onboard, according to Everest Group research, and they're reaping great benefits in terms of business outcomes and a high return on investment. It's no surprise that you'll find a number of vendors ready to help you on your journey. How do you narrow the choice to the right partner?

TIP Start by asking prospective vendors a lot of questions. You want a full understanding of their proposed technology and its capabilities, because you need a proven methodology to gain the best value. You want to learn more about each vendor's track record, including how well its delivery approach works and its ability to handle technological complexity.

Learn more about the vendor's innovation roadmap. You must be certain its technology is headed in the same direction as yours, and be sure it'll be available in the cloud. And get a good look at the ecosystem to gauge the vendor's success. You'll benefit from a mature ecosystem that has partners who can align closely with your requirements.

Asking the right questions

With all that in mind, here's a checklist of questions to ask. (Also be sure to explore Chapter 6 for even more depth into the capabilities you need to consider.)

Checking the capabilities

>> "Is your technology a standalone process mining tool? Or does it also provide automation capabilities?"

>> "Will I be able to extract real-time data into your platform? Will this require a third-party ETL?"

Evaluating the track record

>> "What is the typical deployment time?"

>> "Do you offer pre-packaged software that matches our use cases?"

>> "Please share stories of reference customers — enterprises in a similar industry with a similar technology complexity."

Inquiring about innovation

>> "What is your product roadmap? As your product evolves, which new capabilities will our enterprise be able to benefit from?"

>> "Can you offer tangible examples of how machine learning will be used to improve process execution?"

Exploring the ecosystem

>> "How extensive is your solution's ecosystem? Can a partner deploy the solution on our behalf?"

>> "What are your cloud security accreditations?"

>> "What data governance do you have in place?"

Asking others for insights

There are lots of questions to ask potential vendors, but there are plenty of others to check in with, too, as you explore your options. Other customers as well as analysts can share their perceptions and insights about process mining and execution management. Here are some places to turn:

>> **Reference customers:** Don't just read testimonials; speak with reference customers directly. Your potential vendor should be able to provide you contact info of some customers. Your best bet is to speak with customers in an industry similar to yours, or with similar use cases.

>> **Customer webinars:** If you look around, you're likely to find webinars, panel discussions, and related events in which enterprises sit around and tell their stories. You can get some fantastic insights by hearing how other enterprises are successfully implementing process mining. The closer you get to the kinds of use cases that are common in your world, the better you'll be.

>> **Market analysts:** These experts often conduct webinars about the state of the market. You can hear their perspectives as well as details about customer adoptions. Reach out to the analysts you respect the most to learn about their upcoming events.

>> **Technological experts:** Webinars are great, but you get the most direct, pertinent answers if you can get a briefing directly from a market expert. Ask your potential vendors whom they would recommend contacting.

>> **Technical reports:** The internet is full of analyst reports and whitepapers on all parts of the market and technological innovations. You can buy reports from analysts, and vendors may offer them, too.

Chapter **6**

(More than) Ten Capabilities to Seek in a Process Mining Tool

I f you've turned to this chapter, that probably means you're ready to take the next step and shop for process mining and execution management technology. Read on for some thoughts about what to look for as you evaluate the technology that will serve your business best. Here are a dozen capabilities you need to think about before making a final decision.

Connecting with All Data

It's very important to select a process mining tool that can bring data together, in real time, from all of the necessary sources that will together create a complete picture of your processes. This should include "homegrown" and nonstandard systems, spreadsheets, and other files where process data is stored, along with external data sources.

Ingesting the Data

Once you've identified the data for process mining, you have to get the data into the system, which means critical prerequisites are data preparation, cleaning, and transformation. With that in mind, be sure to check out the suitability of the potential vendor's extract, transform, and load module (ETL). It must meet your data scope.

Checking Out Prebuilt Connectors

Most of the data you'll be using for process mining lives in standard systems, such as SAP, Oracle, and Salesforce. But keep in mind that multisystem is the future in the world of information technology.

Your process mining and execution management tool needs to work with all the right systems, and work with them easily. That means prebuilt connectors that can load data fast, ready-made dashboards, and a selection of analyses already created for you. You shouldn't have to start from scratch.

Excelling at Process Discovery and Intelligence

The process has been mined and the data is in the system. Now's when the insights can start to happen. How good will the insights be that are generated by your process mining technology? It depends.

Pay close attention to the analytics features of the platform, the accessibility to business users, and the availability of pre-configured analytics (such as root cause analysis and process simulation). Carefully evaluate each factor to ensure everything is as exceptional as possible, adequately customizable, and easy to use even if you don't have a data science degree.

Analyzing Complex Processes

The ability to visualize a process is table stakes when it comes to process analytics. You'll need conformance checking and bench-marking tools to compare process performance against the gold standard. Some vendors go above and beyond with advanced features such as process simulation and cross-process analysis.

Enhancing the Processes

Keen insights are absolutely vital, but they're still only part of the story. What good are insights if you can't easily use them to improve your processes?

The ability to execute on the insights you generate from process mining is probably the most important feature of all. At the end of the day, you must be able to enhance your process, or all you've done is conduct an exercise in gloom and frustration. We're talking about the evolution of process mining into execution management, and you'll find this capability built into only a few solutions.

Automating the Process

A key part of enhancement is automation. Whenever you can, you want to remove the need for human actions, and replace them with automated fixes and activities.

By combining process mining with automation, you're able to directly correct process inefficiencies. What will serve your needs best are no-code integrations with ERP systems, cloud tools, and custom software. That's the easiest way to deploy corrective process automation.

Mining for Tasks

As you know, parts of your processes take place outside of transactional IT systems. They often take place on a user's desktop, perhaps in apps such as spreadsheet or email software. That's where *desktop process mining* (DPM), also known as *task mining*, comes into the picture. It lets you capture off-system activities to help improve your process understanding. This, too, is only offered by a small handful of vendors.

Integrating with Existing Tools

Your best business outcomes happen when you create a seamless discovery and enhancement experience. The last thing you want to do is create a complicated new process to learn on top of everything else.

With that in mind, check to see whether process mining can be integrated with your existing technologies such as business intelligence (BI), business process management (BPM), integration platform as a service (iPaaS), and robotic process automation (RPA).

Ensuring Security and Compliance

It's in the headlines just about every morning — another organization held captive to ransomware or embarrassed by a sensitive data breach. Don't be one of those headlines! Sensitive data must be stored and handled securely, whether you keep it on-premise or in the cloud. Your process mining vendor must have strong security policies and accreditations.

Accessing Training and Support

The vendor you choose should provide free and comprehensive training for your team, plus services to help you successfully get up and running with your new process mining tool. The vendor should be ready to help ensure the tool is successfully adopted by your teams.

Connecting with Partners

You probably already work with consulting partners that help you select, deploy, or manage your IT systems. Make sure that your process mining vendor works with those partners, too, and that the vendor offers guidance and certifications to your partners.

Look for a process mining vendor that has a lively and active partner ecosystem, including services partners, technology partners, and independent software vendor partners who are actively building and extending the core tool.